KNOTS for KIDS

BUCK TILTON

Illustrated by Christine Conners

FALCON®

Guilford, Connecticut

An imprint of Globe Pequot, the trade division of
The Rowman & Littlefield Publishing Group, Inc.
4501 Forbes Blvd., Ste. 200
Lanham, MD 20706
www.rowman.com

Distributed by NATIONAL BOOK NETWORK

British Library Cataloguing in Publication Information available

Library of Congress Cataloging-in-Publication Data

Names: Tilton, Buck, author. | Conners, Christine, illustrator.
Title: Knots for kids / Buck Tilton ; illustrated by Christine Conners.
Description: Guilford, Connecticut : FalconGuides, [2022] | Includes index.
 | Audience: Ages 6–10 | Summary: "Outdoor skills expert and veteran
 author Buck Tilton provides readers with accessible information on
 choosing the best knot for each situation, tying different types of
 common knots and hitches, selecting the best kinds of rope, and much
 more. With step-by-step instructions (for both righties and lefties) on
 tying the most used and useful knots, this book teaches children how to
 tie knots like the experts"— Provided by publisher.
Identifiers: LCCN 2021047751 (print) | LCCN 2021047752 (ebook) | ISBN
 9781493059911 (paperback) | ISBN 9781493059928 (epub)
Subjects: LCSH: Knots and splices—Juvenile literature.
Classification: LCC TT840.R66 T55 2022 (print) | LCC TT840.R66 (ebook) |
 DDC 746.42/2—dc23/eng/20211001
LC record available at https://lccn.loc.gov/2021047751
LC ebook record available at https://lccn.loc.gov/2021047752

♾️™ The paper used in this publication meets the minimum requirements of American National Standard for Information Sciences—Permanence of Paper for Printed Library Materials, ANSI/NISO Z39.48-1992.

KNOTS
for
KIDS

We are grateful to the unsung heroes at FalconGuides, who work so hard behind the scenes to make us look better than we really are.

Our sincere thanks to:

Editorial director: David Legere
Production editor: Meredith Dias
Copy editor: Lauren Szalkiewicz
Proofreader: Susan Barnett
Designer: Amanda Wilson
Layout artist: Wendy Reynolds

CONTENTS

INTRODUCTION

If you start with the first knot in this book and work your way through to the last knot, you will learn how to tie a lot. Do you need to know all those knots? Nope. You can do just about everything you need to do with knots if you know six really important ones. Really important knots are called *basic knots* in this book. But even if you don't need to know a lot of them, knots are fun and often useful. And fun and useful are good!

The six basic knots are the figure 8 knot (see page 44), sheet bend (see page 99), bowline (see page 14), rolling hitch (see page 94), constrictor knot (see page 35), and the round turn and two half hitches (see page 95). But you might find another knot or two (or three) that do something you really need— or love—for a knot to do. That's why it's good to work your way through this book, tying as you go.

The knots in this book are in alphabetical order (or, at least, almost alphabetical order). That's so you can find a knot again after you read about it and practice it.

Knots used to hold everything together that needed to be held together. Long before there were hammers and nails, glue, duct tape, or Velcro, there was cordage—and the knots that made it useful. How many knots are there? Well, today that number is greater than 4,000! If you love tying knots, you may be just starting on a long, wonderful journey into the world of knots.

WORDS YOU NEED TO KNOW

You will understand this book a lot better if you know some words and terms that relate specifically to ropes and knots.

If it's fairly big in diameter (say, a third of an inch or bigger) it's usually called a *rope*. If it's smaller, it's usually called a *cord*. If it's really small, it might be *string* or *twine* or *thread*. You fish with *line,* but sometimes ropes and cords are called line, too. And all this stuff lumped together is often called *cordage.*

The *working end* of the rope or cord is the end used to tie a knot. The other end is the *standing end.* In between the working and standing ends lies the *standing part.*

A **bight** is formed when a section of cordage is doubled into a U shape. A bight is the first step in many knots.

BIGHT

LOOP

DRAW LOOP

TURN WITH THE ROPE DOUBLED

ROUND TURN

STOPPER KNOT

BEND

HITCH

A **loop** is formed when a section of cordage is doubled and crosses over itself. Loops are used to start many knots.

A **crossing point** is where the rope or cord crosses itself.

A **draw loop** is created when the working end is not pulled completely through a knot. A draw loop turns the working end into a quick-release device.

A knot that comes undone or untied may also be said to **spill** or **capsize** (a reminder of the nautical history of knots).

To take a wrap around a post or rail is to take a **turn,** but another half-turn around the post or rail creates a **round turn.**

A **stopper** is a knot tied into the end of a rope to prevent it from slipping through a slit, notch, or hole, or to prevent the end of rope from fraying (coming apart). Stoppers are sometimes tied as simple backups for more complex knots to keep the complex knots from spilling.

A **bend** is a joining knot, one that joins or "bends" two separate ropes or cords together to form one rope or cord.

A **hitch** is used to attach a rope to a post, pile, ring, rail, another line, or even to itself—or to attach something to a rope.

KNOT TYING TIPS

Choose the simplest knot that will get the job done for you. It will be easiest to learn, easiest to remember, quickest to tie, and usually the easiest to untie.

Practice in order to tie all knots correctly. Many knots can be tied more than one way. The way you tie a knot doesn't matter, but the way the knot ends up is very, very important. If all the loops and turns are not in the right place at the end, the knot might not work.

Knots can be tied right-handed or left-handed, depending on whether you are right-handed or left-handed. A knot tied right-handed will be the mirror image of the same knot tied left-handed, and they both will work.

A properly tied knot must be properly tightened. Most knots must be slowly tightened—shaped, kneaded, molded, coaxed—into the proper shape.

When tightening any knot, follow this guideline: Work snug and then tighten. Take out the slack a little at a time, removing it from both the working and the standing ends. Last of all, give it a tightening tug.

THE
KNOTS

ALPINE BUTTERFLY

FORMS A FIXED LOOP IN THE STANDING PART OF A ROPE

This knot creates a fixed loop (a loop that will not move). You can tie it at any place in a rope. It's a loop you can clip or tie just about anything to, including a person. It is especially popular in glacier travel, where it's common to find three climbers attached to one rope, one climber at each end and one in the middle. Unlike the loop knot (see page 76), the alpine butterfly will safely hold up with a lot of weight attached. It stands up to being pulled from either direction without weakening.

In addition to strength and security, the alpine butterfly almost always unties easily, even after being heavily weighted. Other loops can get so tight you'll never get them untied. As with other loops, you can use this knot to make a rope with a weak spot stronger. To strengthen a rope, tie this knot with the weak spot in the loop of the butterfly.

Like a lot of knots, this one can be tied in several different ways. This way is not very difficult.

Wrap the rope around your left hand twice, as shown in the photograph.

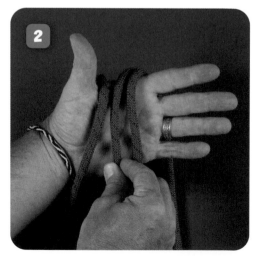

Move the turn closest to your fingertips to lie between the other two turns.

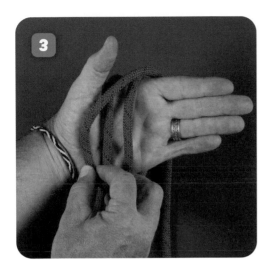

Move the turn that is now closest to your fingertips to lie closest to your thumb.

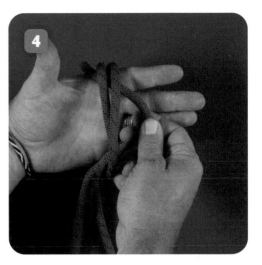

Bring the turn now closest to your thumb underneath the other two turns toward your fingertips. By grasping the loop, you can now remove the rope from your hand.

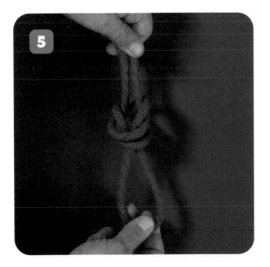

Shape the knot by pulling on the loop and the two main sections of the rope.

Tighten the knot by pulling on the two main sections of the rope.

ANCHOR (FISHERMAN'S) BEND

A RELATIVELY STRONG AND SECURE HITCH, ESPECIALLY FOR WET OR SLICK LINES

The anchor bend (also known as the fisherman's bend) is another knot that got stuck with the wrong name. It is actually a *hitch*, handy for jobs like tying the mooring lines of small boats to mooring rings. It's a strong knot, and it works well in lines slippery from wetness or slippery because of the material the rope is made from. Polypropylene ropes are very slippery. The anchor bend is a variation of the round turn and two half hitches (see page 95). This knot works well when you want to hang something from the limb of a tree.

Take the working end of the line over or through the anchoring point.

Take the working end around or through the anchoring point a second time.

Really Love Knots?

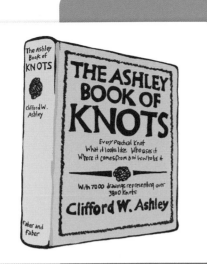

The Ashley Book of Knots by Clifford W. Ashley was written in 1944 and contains over 3,800 knots! It took Mr. Ashley eleven years to write and it has never gone out of print!

Bring the working end across the standing part and through both turns in the line that is around or through the anchoring point. You have now tied a half hitch through two loops.

Snug up the first half hitch and tie a second half hitch around the standing part. Tighten the entire knot.

ASHER'S BOTTLE SLING

USED FOR HANGING A BOTTLE OR OTHER SIMILAR CONTAINER OF LIQUID

Onboard a ship, bottles of liquid—water, stove fuel, juice—can slip, slide, fall, spill, or break open. This is a sling knot that grips the necks of many containers (not just glass) allowing you to hang a container safely or carry it easier. But you don't have to be on a boat to use this knot. Sling knots may also be useful to anyone who wants to secure a container of liquid for ease of carrying, hanging, or hauling.

Begin by tying a piece of twine or cord into the appropriate-size loop. A fine knot for tying a loop is the fisherman's double knot (see page 60). Lay the loop beneath the neck of the bottle.

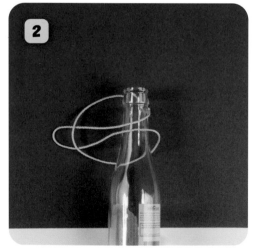

Bring the bight on one side across the neck and through the bight on the other side, as shown in the photograph.

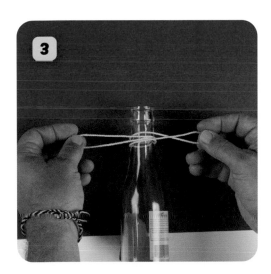

Bring the outer bight across the neck and give it a half twist into a loop.

Bring the inner bight under the neck of the bottle and through the loop. Tighten by pulling on the inner bight and adjust the whole knot until it seats tightly against the neck.

ASHLEY'S STOPPER KNOT

A BULKY STOPPER TO BLOCK HOLES OR SLOTS WHEN SMALLER STOPPERS PULL FREE

When you need a knot to stop a rope from running through a hole or notch, and overhands and figure 8 knots are too small, Ashley's stopper knot does the job. It gets bigger by bringing the working end back into the knot before the final tightening. This is one of those knots named for the person who invented it. Clifford W. Ashley, author of *The Ashley Book of Knots*, created this knot.

Tie a slipknot—a simple sliding loop (see page 101)—in the working end.

Bring the working end through the back of the sliding loop. For the best results, tighten the overhand knot before bringing the working end through the loop. Then tighten the sliding loop by pulling on the standing part to create the three overlapping strands, as shown in the photograph.

BODY KNOT

1. Place the rope in front of you on a flat surface.

2. Fold your arms so that your right hand is resting on top and your left hand is underneath your other arm. Pick up the rope with your right hand.

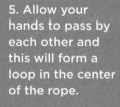

3. With arms still folded, pick up the other end of the rope with your left hand that is still resting below.

4. Slowly uncross your arms while still holding onto the rope.

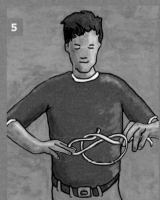

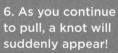

5. Allow your hands to pass by each other and this will form a loop in the center of the rope.

6. As you continue to pull, a knot will suddenly appear!

BACHMANN HITCH

A FRICTION KNOT FOR ASCENDING A ROPE WITH A CARABINER

The Bachmann hitch attaches a carabiner to a rope with strong cord or webbing so that the carabiner can be used as a handle. (Carabiners, by the way, are worth tossing in your rope bag, even if you aren't a climber.) Without a load, this hitch slides freely up the rope. Once weight is applied, the hitch grips the rope, preventing the load from slipping back down the rope. The greater the difference between the diameter of the cord of the hitch and the diameter of the main rope, the greater the grip of the hitch. This knot could be used to hang a load from a vertically suspended rope, such as hanging a food bag while camping.

KNOT CARD GAME (1+ PLAYERS)
Write the name of the knots you learned from this book onto 3x5 index cards. With a group of friends, or alone, flip over the name on the card and test your skills to see if you know how to tie that knot!

Attach a carabiner to a loop and place the loop around the rope, as shown in the photograph. (You can tie a loop with the fisherman's double knot on page 60.)

Bring the end of the loop around the rope and through the carabiner.

Bring the end of the loop around the rope and through the carabiner a second time.

Bring the end of the loop around the rope and through the carabiner a third time. If the hitch does not grip adequately, you may add another turn of the loop. The knot must finish with the loop pulled out through the carabiner.

BACKSPLICE

A KNOT THAT INTERWEAVES THE STRANDS OF A BRAIDED ROPE TO PREVENT FRAYING

Traditionally, ropes were made of three strands of fiber twisted together. When the rope was cut to the required length, splicing was required to prevent fraying. Being able to backsplice a rope was considered a basic skill required of anyone who handled a lot of rope. Some ropes are made with four strands, but this same method of backsplicing will work with four strands. Because backsplicing serves the same purpose as whipping (tying smaller stuff around a cut end of rope to prevent fraying), this knot is sometimes known as Spanish whipping. Unlike whipping (see page 118), your backsplice will actually become stronger with use.

Begin by interweaving the loose strands into a knot known as a crown, as shown in the photograph. Do this by forming a bight in each strand, then tucking the end of the adjacent strand through the bight. Work clockwise around the unraveled end of the rope.

Tighten the crown knot against the end of the rope. Splicing can start now.

Knots to Count By

Ancient Incas in Peru used a knot system called quipu to count and record information about farming, taxes, dates, and statistics. The system used various types of knots tied on numerous cords of various colors. North American Indians were also known to use knots to record and calculate dates!

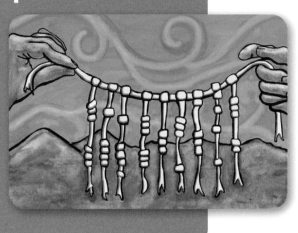

Lead one strand against the lay of the rope (the direction of the twists of the strands). Go over the next strand and under the third strand. Do this with all three strands, making sure the strands leave the crown at regular intervals, each strand centered on approximately one-third of the circumference of the rope.

Continue to weave the three strands against the lay of the rope, over and under, until each strand is tucked back into the rope two or three times. You can trim off the end of the strand—which is a good idea—but do not trim them too short, because the splice can unravel. Roll the splice between your hands to make it neat and round.

BOWLINE

A FIXED LOOP AT THE END OF A LINE OR FOR ATTACHING A LINE TO AN OBJECT

The bowline, one of the basic knots, is one of the most famous of all knots. It creates a fixed loop that does not slip or jam. It is, however, far from being a secure knot. It can be shaken loose when unloaded, and it has been known to capsize or deform when overloaded. It is, therefore, best backed up with a stopper (see the final photograph). But even while loaded, this knot can be untied by pushing up on the bight that surrounds the standing part. When a loop has to be untied later, the bowline is a great choice. It is useful in jobs big and small, from securing string before tying a package to securing a gear bag to be hauled up a cliff by climbers. The size of the loop, from very small to very large, is determined by you, the tyer. More trustworthy variations of the bowline, such as the double bowline (see page 18) and the triple bowline (see page 20), are also in this book.

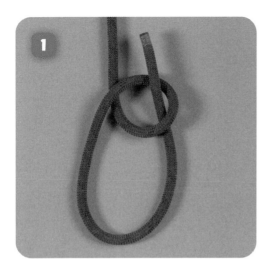

Form a small loop in the standing part of the line and bring the working end back up through the loop, as shown in the photograph.

Take the working end around behind the standing part and back down through the loop. Pull slowly on the standing part to form the knot—but do not tighten the knot.

Adjust the main loop to the required size, and tighten the knot.

Finish with an overhand stopper (see page 86) to add security to the bowline.

BOWLINE ON A BIGHT

A FIXED DOUBLE LOOP THAT CAN BE TIED IN THE MIDDLE OF A LINE

Bowline on a bight, bowline in the bight, bowline upon the bight—they are all names for the same knot. This knot can be tied near a working end of a rope but more often appears away from an end. In the old days, this knot was used as an improvised seat, the seated person shoving one leg through one loop, the other leg through the other loop. The person in the seat held onto the line and was then lowered or raised, such as up or down the side of a ship. When a double loop is tied in the middle of a rope, a weight (such as a person) can be lowered or raised from two points, allowing for more security and control during the process. Because devices such as harnesses now exist to aid in moving a person with a rope, the bowline on a bight is not recommended for such use except in emergencies. You can use it to tie gear to the middle of a rope.

FUN FACT

Tying our shoelaces is the first knot most of us learned!

With the line doubled, form a loop in the doubled line as if a basic bowline (see page 14) was being tied.

Take the double end up through the loop, again as if a basic bowline was being tied.

Take the end of the single loop down and around the end of the double loop.

Continue to bring the end of the single loop over the knot that has now been created in the line. Adjust the size of the double loop to the desired dimension before tightening.

BOWLINE (DOUBLE)

A VARIATION OF THE BASIC BOWLINE THAT ADDS SECURITY TO THE KNOT

A second loop at the beginning of a double bowline doubles the pressure on the working end, and that gives you a stronger knot. The finished knot does *not* have two loops, even though the name might make you think it does. If you need a double loop, use the bowline on a bight (see page 16). All things considered, it is an overall stronger knot than the basic bowline or the bowline on a bight. A stopper knot in the working end also adds security.

Form a loop in the working end of the rope as if a basic bowline (see page 14) was being tied.

Form a second loop, a duplicate of the first loop, and lay it on top of the first loop.

Knots were used by early humans to survive. Using plant fibers and animal skins, early humans created ropes and used them to create knots to catch animals, design weapons, and build shelters.

Bring the working end up through both loops and in back of the standing part as if tying a basic bowline.

Bring the working end down through both loops and tighten the knot. As with the basic bowline, a stopper knot in the working end adds even more security.

BOWLINE (TRIPLE)

A FIXED TRIPLE LOOP THAT CREATES A MORE SECURE EMERGENCY "CHAIR"

The triple bowline is no more than a basic bowline tied on a long bight in a way that creates three loops. Because it is tied on a bight, it can be tied in the middle of a rope if that's where you want it. With a lot of fidgety work, the size of each loop can be adjusted to differing sizes. This allows the knot to be used as a chair (with each of two loops around someone's legs and the third loop around the body under the arms). As with other knots used as chairs, the triple bowline is recommended only when no other means of raising or lowering a person is available. This knot sees very little use today, but it is highly useful when it is needed.

BLIND KNOT TYING
Check your mastery of a knot you just learned by closing your eyes and tying it without looking.

1

2

Make a long bight in the rope and form a loop as if you're starting to tie a basic bowline (see page 14).

Take the doubled end up through the loop and around, behind the standing part.

3

4

Take the doubled end back down through the loop. (At this point, you are on your way to tying a bowline on a bight.)

The doubled end becomes the third of three loops in the finished knot. Adjust the size of the loops, and tighten the knot.

BULL HITCH

A STRONGER, "BEEFIER" VARIATION ON THE COW HITCH

The bull hitch is sort of like the cow hitch (see page 38) and the pedigree cow hitch (see page 40). The bull hitch stays tied better, but it is a bit more difficult to tie. Because the bull hitch tends to jam if the standing part is heavily loaded, especially by a sudden jerk, it is most often used as a temporary tether and not in situations where it will be left alone for a long time.

Drape the working end of a rope over a rail or bar and bring it across the front of the standing part.

Wrap the working end in a complete turn around the standing part of the rope.

Bring the working end up and over the rail or bar (from the back) a second time (as shown in the photograph).

Take the working end down through the loop in the knot through which the standing part passes. Tighten by pulling on the standing part.

BUNTLINE HITCH

A VERY SECURE CHOICE WHEN THE KNOT WILL BE SHAKEN VIGOROUSLY

The buntline hitch is a kind of sliding loop, because it slides on the line after being tied, but you can use it when you need a hitch. It could be described as a clove hitch (see page 32) with the working end tied around the standing part. On sailing ships, the buntline was attached to the bottom of sails so they could be drawn up to spill the wind. Because it does sometimes jam, do not use this knot when the hitch needs to be untied quickly. But if you need a knot that won't come untied, such as in a high wind, this one does the job.

OBSERVATION GAME (1+ PLAYERS)
On your next visit to nature, bring a lariat (see directions on page 27) and a magnifying glass. Walk with your lariat loop tossing randomly on the ground. Using your magnifying glass, see how many tiny and amazing things you can find inside the loop!

1. Take the working end of the rope through or around the attachment point and back across the standing part to form a loop.

2. Bring the working end fully around the standing part.

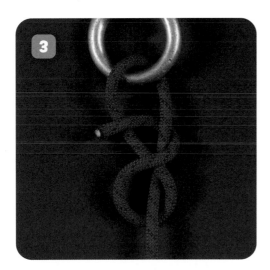

3. Take the working end around and through the loop from the back, as shown in the photograph.

4. Tuck the working end back through the knot, forming a half hitch. The final tuck of the working end within the knot makes the buntline hitch work. Tighten the knot, then pull the standing part to snug the knot against the attachment point.

CAMEL HITCH

A HITCH FOR SITUATIONS WHERE THE PULL MIGHT BE APPLIED IN ANY DIRECTION FROM THE KNOT

The camel hitch makes an excellent knot choice when what you've tied to the hitch might shift from one direction to another. You know, like a horse—or, yes, a camel. It can be used to attach a smaller line to a larger one. Whether wet or dry, you can untie it easily. This knot is used in camping, for example, when tying a tent line to a stake.

With the working end, make two full turns around the bar, rail, or other attachment point.

Take the working end across the front of the standing part, around the attachment point, and down through itself twice, as shown in the photograph. Work the completed hitch tight by pulling on the working end and standing part simultaneously. For greater security, make the last two turns into two half hitches (see page 64), one tight against the other.

THE LARIAT

The lariat is a device commonly used by cowboys to lasso and tether cattle. The lariat uses a stiff rope and a honda knot to create a sliding loop that could be used for a variety of purposes.

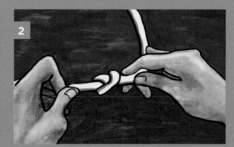

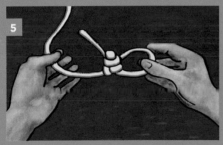

1. Tie a tight overhand knot at the end of a stiff 20- to 30-foot rope (to act as a stopper).

2. Create a second overhand knot but keep this knot loose.

3. Take the first knotted end and pull it through the loosened knot.

4. Pull the side of the loop to tighten it up, but don't let the stopper knot slide through!

5. Pull tightly.

6. Now pass the other end of the rope through to create your lasso!

CARRICK BEND

A KNOT USED FOR JOINING TWO LARGE LINES SECURELY

The carrick bend creates a very stable knot when tied correctly, even when the material in the two lines differs, such as when synthetic ropes are tied to natural-fiber ropes. But this knot is often tied incorrectly by beginning knot tyers. Follow the directions carefully until you know the knot. The wrongly tied knot appears, on casual glance, to be a carrick bend, but it spills under pressure. Because of this, some knot enthusiasts refer to the knot pictured here as the *true* carrick bend.

Make a loop in the working end of the first line.

Lay the working end of the second line across the first loop, as shown in the photograph.

OLD WEST COWBOY GAME

Once you've created your own lasso, set up a chair or standing object in your yard or park. Give each player three tries to loop the lasso around the object!

Bring the second working end around the back of the standing part of the first line, then over the first working end. Then bring it behind the first loop but over its own standing part where it crosses under the first loop, as shown in the photograph.

Tighten the knot slowly by pulling on both standing parts. As the knot tightens, it will form the shape shown in the final, upper photograph. The working ends on the opposite sides of the knot create a stronger union than when the ends emerge on the same side of the knot.

CHAIN SINNET (MONKEY CHAIN)

A NEAT WAY TO STORE SHORT PIECES OF ROPE

All chain sinnets—and there are several—have this in common: loops, one after another, tucked into each other. When you're done, this chain sinnet (also called a monkey chain) works great as a method of packing short pieces of cord or rope in a way that prevents tangling. You don't want to do this with a really long rope, because it would take forever. You can also use a chain sinnet to shorten a cord, like a long pull cord on a curtain.

Form a loop in the cord.

Tuck a second loop of the cord through the first loop as shown in the photograph. An overhand knot with draw loop has now been tied in the cord.

Ancient Egyptians used ropes and knots to pull stones through the desert and to lift them into place. They also used them to secure the tombs of pharaohs and to support their ships' masts.

3

Tuck a third loop through the second loop. At this point begin to tighten and arrange the loops as you go along. Note: No tightening is necessary if the cord or rope is being prepared for packing or storage.

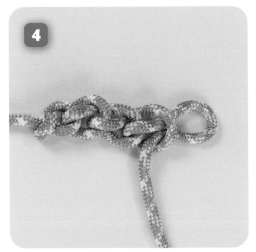

4

Continue to add loops to the sinnet until you reach the desired length. Thread the working end through the final loop to lock the knot.

CLOVE HITCH

ONE OF THE BEST KNOWN AND MOST WIDELY USED HITCHES

This knot is one of the most all-around useful of all quick hitches for all kinds of jobs. The simple beauty of the clove hitch, though, might make you forget that over time, especially if the pull on the rope is not at a right angle to the point of attachment, it will come untied.

Wrap the working end of the rope around an object, laying it over the standing part as shown in the photograph.

Wrap the working end around the object a second time and underneath the crossed-over section of the first turn. Tighten by pulling simultaneously on the working end and standing end, taking care to keep the distinctive shape of the knot.

CLOVE HITCH ON A RING

A VARIATION OF THE CLOVE HITCH USED FOR TYING A ROPE TO A RING

This method of tying a clove hitch to a ring or similar object allows the knot to be easily loosened and retightened to control the length of the rope leading to the ring. It is commonly used by anyone in just about any circumstance who needs a quick, temporary hitch.

Feed the working end of the rope through the ring from behind and bring it down and behind the standing part.

Bring the working end up through the ring again (from the back) and down through the back of the bight of the knot, as shown in the photograph. Tighten by pulling on the standing part.

CLOVE HITCH ON A STAKE

A VARIATION OF THE CLOVE HITCH USED FOR TYING A ROPE TO A STAKE

This method of tying a clove hitch allows the rope to be dropped quickly over a stake or post and tightened instead of tying the knot around the object. As a bonus, it can be tied at any point in a rope—such as in the middle of a very long length of cordage.

Form two loops in a rope, one in the right hand, one in the left, as shown in the photograph.

Place the right-hand loop on top of the left-hand loop. Drop the two loops over a stake and tighten by pulling simultaneously on both ends of the rope, taking care to maintain the distinctive shape of the hitch.

CONSTRICTOR KNOT

A BINDING KNOT THAT SIMPLY DOES NOT COME UNDONE

Here is another basic knot. This is a really great knot when you want the knot to just about never come untied. Once you pull this knot really tight, it can refuse to come undone. When fully tightened, it might be easier to cut it off than untie it. When you want this knot to keep doing its job for a long time, the rope or cord can be trimmed off short on both sides of the knot.

With the working end of the line, tie a clove hitch (see page 32) around the attachment point.

Tuck the working end under the first turn of the clove hitch and tighten. Note: When the knot will need to be untied, the final tuck can be made as a draw loop (see page 87).

CONSTRICTOR KNOT (DOUBLE)

A VARIATION OF THE CONSTRICTOR KNOT THAT BINDS EVEN MORE SECURELY

When you want a super-binding knot, the double constrictor, the best of all binding knots, cannot be beat. It has been compared to the grip of a boa constrictor. When the diameter of whatever this knot is tied to is large, the basic constrictor knot (see page 35) loses some of its strength—and that's when you want the double constrictor. It can be used, for example, as a substitute for hose clamps. With a short length of cord, the double constrictor knot works great to hold a sack without a drawstring closed. This knot works really well for attaching cords to the handles of tools, or anything else of similar design, to allow them to be hung. It can be used to attach a pencil to a clipboard.

Take the working end of the line around the object and across itself.

Take the working end around the object and across itself a second time, maintaining the diagonal direction as shown in the photograph.

Bring the working end over the standing part and tuck it under the pair of diagonal turns as shown in the photograph.

Tuck the working end under the remaining single turn and tighten by working all the slack out of the knot.

COW HITCH (SIMPLE)

ANOTHER QUICK AND SIMPLE, THOUGH INSECURE, GENERAL-PURPOSE HITCH

Sometimes snobby knot tyers scoff at the simple cow hitch because it's, well, so simple. Plus, it loosens easily due to the fact that the weight of a load pulls entirely on the standing part of the rope, which means there's no pressure to hold the knot itself together. It is often used to temporarily tether animals, like cows, but don't use this knot for a long period of time.

Drape the working end of a rope through a ring, as shown in the photograph, or over a rail or bar.

Bring the working end across the front of the standing part, back up and through the ring or over the rail again, and down through the bight of the knot, as shown in the photograph. Tighten by pulling on the standing part.

Celtic Knot

Celtic knots are sometimes called endless or mystic knots. They are thought to have their origins in the late Roman Empire and can be found on Roman floor mosaics, illuminated manuscripts, crosses, architecture, jewelry, and in Ethiopian and Islamic art. Thought to represent the eternal circle of life, Celtic knot designs consist of endless interwoven ribbons that have no clear beginning or end. In the era of Christianity, Celtic knots became a symbol of protection against evil forces who were thought to become frustrated by the endless nature and constant movement of the designs.

COW HITCH (PEDIGREE)

A VARIATION OF THE SIMPLE COW HITCH THAT MAKES A MORE RELIABLE KNOT

By tucking the working end of the rope back into the simple cow hitch (see page 38), the pedigree cow hitch is created. That one tuck turns a lightweight and undependable knot into a fairly secure and serviceable knot with numerous uses. And, unlike the simple cow hitch, a load can be applied to the pedigree cow hitch from any angle, making it close to ideal for tethering just about any animal. It is a handy knot for suspending tools or other items from pegs or crossbeams over patios or in garages, sheds, or other storage areas.

Drape the working end of a rope over a rail or bar, as shown in the photograph.

Bring the working end across the front of the standing part.

Bring the working end back up and over the rail again, and down through the bight of the knot, as shown in the photograph.

Tuck the working end behind both turns of the rope that go around the rail or bar. Tighten by pulling on the standing part.

EYE SPLICE

USED TO CREATE AN EYE AT THE END OF A ROPE

Being able to create an "eye," or a loop, at the end of a rope was once considered an important skill for people who used ropes a lot, especially sailors. Although now you can buy ropes with eyes at the end, a reliable one can be made with this technique. It only works with ropes that are braided (ropes made of several strands of material twisted or braided together). You will probably need a tool, like a screwdriver, to work the strands apart. Tucking the strands three times works well with fiber ropes, but synthetic material, being slippery, requires five tucks to be secure. Finish the splice with tape, whipping, or heat (with synthetic material) to further secure it.

Unlay the end of a rope (separate the strands) and form an eye of the required size. Tuck the end of one loose strand under a strand in the standing part. Tuck the next loose strand under the next strand in the standing part.

Turn the rope over and tuck the third loose strand under the only strand in the standing part that has yet to be used. Repeat the process until each loose strand has been tucked into the standing part three times. Roll the splice between your hands to achieve the proper shape.

HEART KNOTS

Heart knots are fun and simple to tie! They can be used to make a necklace or given as gifts to family and friends.

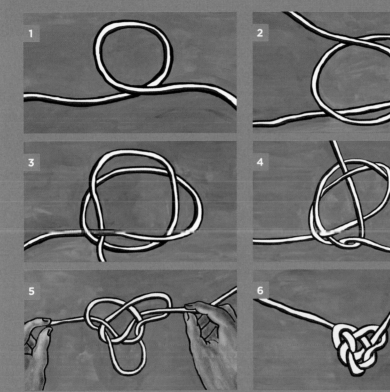

1. Start with 3 feet of thin rope or paracord. Create a loop in the center of the cord. The cord on your right will be your working cord. Leave the one on the left stationary. (You may want to tape it down.)

2. Take the cord on your right and place it back under the loop, through the loop, and then over the loop.

3. Curve your working cord back around and weave it under and over the lower loops as shown.

4. Curve your working cord back again, under and then over through the loops as shown.

5. Gently pull the two cords apart to close the knot.

6. Patiently shape and pinch the bottom of the knot until it looks like a heart!

FIGURE 8 KNOT

A QUICK, EFFICIENT, AND ATTRACTIVE STOPPER KNOT

The figure 8 knot is a basic knot and one of the most useful knots. Some knot experts call this knot the best overall knot to know. By itself, it doesn't work a whole lot better than a simple overhand. What it does do is untie easier than an overhand, and so it works well when a stopper needs to be tied and untied often. The figure 8 forms the basis for many other knots and is, therefore, a knot you need to know. It can be changed when it's tied (keep reading this book) to work as a bend, loop, or hitch.

THE HUMAN KNOT GAME (6–10 PLAYERS)
Each person grabs the hands of two different players that are not directly next to them to create a tangled human knot. The goal of the game is to try to then untangle the knot without letting go of their hands (except to prevent injury).

Form a loop in the working end of a rope.

Twist the end of the loop to form a second loop.

Bring the working end of the rope up through the second loop.

Tighten the knot by pulling on both the working end and the standing part. Notice the characteristic figure 8 shape that gives this knot its name.

FIGURE 8 LOOP

A STRONG AND SECURE FIXED LOOP FOR ALL DIAMETERS OF CORDAGES

The figure 8 loop is one of the most widely known and used loops. It's easy to tie and works well in diameters of cordage ranging from thin thread to thick rope. It also ranks high as a secure loop: Once tied, it stays tied. But if you want to be even more sure this knot stays tied, finish it with a stopper knot in the working end, a procedure that will get rid of any chance the figure 8 could slip. A stopper can be added with ease if the working end is left long enough. Those who argue against the stopper point out that the figure 8 loop, after being weighted, often proves difficult, but not impossible, to undo.

Create a large bight in the working end and double it over to form a loop.

Bring the doubled working end over the doubled standing part.

Artist Ed Bing Lee is "knot" your average artist! Ed Bing Lee is a knot artist who's been making knot art for over forty years! Using various knot techniques, he's created fun and creative knot art including the ice cream cone you see at left. The ice cream cone is a part of a series of twelve images that depict the typical and most popular foods of Americana cuisine! The ice cream cone made with waxed linen and linen cord is 6x6x6 inches in size, and was made using a double half hitch, wrapping, and a single hitch. Check out the rest of the meal here: edbinglee.net.

Bring the doubled working end up through the original loop.

Tighten slowly by pulling on the loop and the main standing part to create the characteristic figure 8.

FIGURE 8 KNOT WITH DRAW LOOP

A VARIATION OF THE FIGURE 8 KNOT THAT IS MUCH EASIER TO UNTIE

The figure 8 with draw loop is a great choice when you'll need the knot for a little while. This knot releases quickly, as any draw loop does, by pulling on the working end. The addition of the draw loop increases the size of the standard figure 8 if you need a larger stopper.

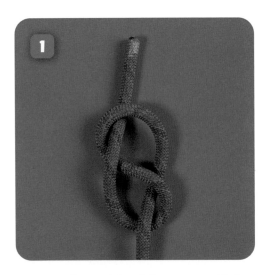

Create a figure 8 knot (see page 44) in the working end of a rope, but do not tighten the knot.

Bring the working end back through the upper loop of the figure 8 but only far enough to form the draw loop. Tighten the knot by pulling on the loop and the standing part.

SIMPLE NECKTIE KNOT

Nothing says you mean business like the necktie! The idea for neckties is thought to have originated with Croatian soldiers who served as mercenaries in France during the Thirty Years' War (1618–1648). Their stylish uniforms were accentuated by pieces of knotted cloth worn around their necks. Parisians, and even King Louis XIII, took note of this handsome accessory and adopted it as their own.

1. Place the tie around your neck.

2. Cross the wide end over the thin end.

3. Pass the wide end behind the thin end and back over your hand.

4. Pull the wide end around your hand and up through the backside of the big loop.

5. Pull the wide end through the loop created by your hand.

6. Pull the wide end all the way through and tighten it up by sliding the knot up to the collar. Now you're ready for business!

FIGURE 8 DOUBLE LOOP

A VARIATION OF THE FIGURE 8 THAT CREATES TWIN LOOPS IN THE ROPE

The figure 8 double loop (sometimes called "bunny ears") creates twin loops that allow you to tie one rope to two anchors, something you might do if you're serious about climbing. Once you've got it down, this knot ties quickly and forms two fixed loops. A fixed loop will not change in size when weight is applied to either or both loops. If loops of differing sizes are needed, however, the loops can be adjusted to different sizes during the tying—and they, too, will not change in size.

Form a large bight in the rope and twist the bight into a loop as if starting a simple figure 8 (see page 44).

Reach through the loop and grasp the doubled rope, as shown in the photograph.

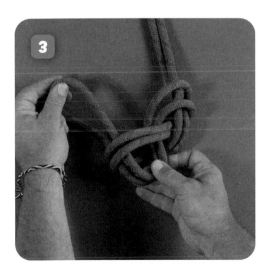

Bring the doubled rope through the loop as if tying a figure 8 with draw loop (see page 48). The doubled section of rope pulled through the loop will become the double loop.

Bring the remaining single loop down in front of the knot, take the doubled loops through the single loop, and move the single loop up to the top of the knot. Carefully tighten everything.

FIGURE 8 TRIPLE LOOP

A VARIATION OF THE FIGURE 8 THAT CREATES THREE LOOPS IN THE ROPE

The figure 8 triple loop creates three loops that allow you to attach one rope to three anchors—something you might want to do if you're a really serious climber. Once you know how to tie it, this knot forms three fixed loops that will not change in size once the final knot is tightened. As with the triple bowline (see page 20), the figure 8 triple loop could be used in an emergency as a chair sling to raise or lower a person, with one loop for each leg and the third loop around the body of the person beneath the armpits. Don't use this knot on a person unless you don't have anything else to use.

Form a large bight in the rope and twist the bight into a loop as if starting a simple figure 8 (see page 46).

Reach through the loop and grasp the doubled rope. Bring the doubled rope through the loop as if tying a figure 8 with draw loop (see page 48). You are now at a point where you could tie a figure 8 double loop (see page 50).

Some snakes will tie themselves into knots to protect themselves from predators or to help them shed their skin.

Bring the remaining single loop over the top of the knot.

Bring this loop down through the original loop to create three loops. Carefully tighten everything. (The three loops in the photograph are smaller than most people would need but are shown small for photographic purposes.)

FIGURE 8 FOLLOW-THROUGH

A FIXED LOOP, THE STANDARD TIE-IN KNOT FOR CLIMBERS

This is the usual tie-in knot for climbers. The tie-in knot is where a climber is attached to a climbing rope. If you're a climber, you need to be totally sure you've tied this one right. If you fall, you depend on the rope, and the knot, to save your life. If you can know only one knot well, beginning climbers are often told, the figure 8 follow-through is the one. Before trusting this knot to save your life, leave enough working end to back up the knot with a stopper. The overhand double (see page 86) is an excellent choice as stopper.

BLINDFOLDED KNOT GAME (2+ PLAYERS)
Players will take turns either being the knot tyer or blindfolded. Using the knots from the book, one player ties a chosen knot, and the blindfolded player has to guess which knot they are holding using only their hands!

Tie a figure 8 knot (see page 44) in the working end of the rope. You will need this knot to be 2 to 3 feet from the end of the rope.

With the working end, begin to trace, or follow the lead of, the first figure 8, as shown in the photograph.

Continue to follow the lead of the figure 8.

The working end needs to come out of the knot in line with the standing part, as shown in the photograph.

FIGURE 8 BEND

A MORE COMPLEX KNOT USED FOR SECURELY JOINING TWO ROPES OF SIMILAR SIZE AND CONSTRUCTION

A bend, remember, is a knot for tying two ropes together. The figure 8 bend is tied by weaving together two figure 8 knots. Many people who want to tie two ropes together use this knot. Climbers like it a lot because it is very strong and not easy to untie. If heavily loaded, this knot may prove impossible to untie if the ropes are of approximately the same diameter. It doesn't work well if the two ropes are different in diameter. Despite its security, climbers often leave the working ends long enough to back up the knot with stoppers, adding even more security (not a bad idea when your life may depend on your knot).

Tie a figure 8 knot (see page 44) in the working end of one rope.

Thread the working end of the second rope into the figure 8 knot in the first rope, as shown in the photograph.

Continue to follow the lead of the first rope. The goal is to create a second figure 8 knot that duplicates but is a mirror image of the first figure 8 knot.

When both ropes have been woven into one figure 8 knot, carefully compress and tighten the composite knot into the characteristic figure 8 shape. For the greatest strength, make sure the standing part of both ropes forms the outer bight at both ends of the knot.

FISHERMAN'S KNOT

A SIMPLE KNOT FOR JOINING TWO ROPES OR CORDS OF SIMILAR DIAMETER

You don't have to be a fisherman to use this knot. But because it works very well in lines of very small diameter, such as fishing line, it is popular with people who fish. That's why it's called a fisherman's knot, as you probably guessed. It's simple and easy to tie. This knot combines two overhand knots that jam against each other when you pull on the two ropes being tied together. And it unties fairly easily, even after being weighted, but it can bind up and be hard to untie if it gets jerked tight suddenly. The knot works best in ropes of similar thickness and, therefore, does a fine job of tying two ends of the same rope or cord together. It's a perfect knot for tying a short piece of rope into a permanent loop.

Form an overhand knot at the working end of the first rope.

Thread the working end of the second rope through the overhand knot in the first rope, as shown in the photograph.

Tie an overhand knot in the working end of the second rope. The second overhand must be tied around the first rope, as shown in the photograph.

Tighten both overhand knots and draw them together slowly by pulling on the standing parts of both ropes.

FISHERMAN'S DOUBLE KNOT

ONE OF THE SAFEST, MOST SECURE KNOTS FOR JOINING TWO ROPES OF SIMILAR DIAMETER

Yes, the fisherman's double knot, or double fisherman's knot, is twice the size—and twice the strength—of a fisherman's knot. When you join two ropes or lines of similar size with this knot, they are very securely joined. In the double fisherman's, two overhand double knots jam against each other when pressure is applied. It is an excellent choice when using synthetic cordage, including fishing line. It works in natural-fiber cordage, of course, but it can become extremely difficult to untie from anything other than synthetics. When this knot is tied correctly, it stays put.

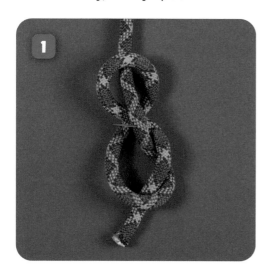

Tie an overhand double knot (see page 86) at the working end of the first rope.

Thread the working end of the second rope through both loops of the overhand double knot in the first rope, as shown in the photograph.

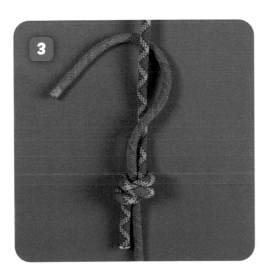

Tighten the overhand double in the first rope.

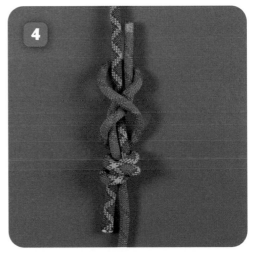

At this point it will be easier to continue if you reverse the knot assembly in your hand. Tie an overhand double in the working end of the second rope, making sure both loops of the knot are around the standing part of the first rope. Tighten the second overhand double and draw both knots together slowly by pulling on the standing part of both ropes.

GARDA KNOT

A RATCHETING KNOT THAT USES TWO CARABINERS AND IS USEFUL IN HAULING

The Garda knot ratchets, which means the rope can pass through a pair of carabiners in one direction only. The two carabiners should be the same size and shape, and they should *not* be locking carabiners, because the locks prevent them from pinching the rope firmly enough for the knot to work.

Clip two carabiners into a sling, side by side, with the gates facing in the same direction. Pass the rope through both carabiners and form a loop, as shown in the photograph.

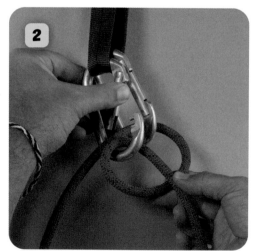

Pass the loop through the first carabiner only. Slide the loop onto the spines of the carabiners, the sides opposite to the gates, before putting weight on the rope.

GIRTH HITCH

USED FOR QUICKLY ATTACHING A LOOP TO ANY OBJECT

Simple and fast to tie, the girth hitch (or ring hitch) has many uses. It attaches a pre-sewn or pre-tied loop or sling to almost any object. It can be used to connect loops. Climbers often use a girth hitch in slings of webbing, but it works in any type of rope or cordage.

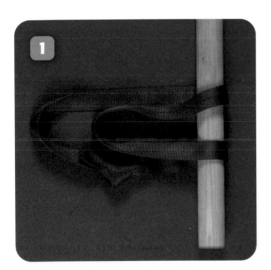

Pass the loop around the object to which it is to be attached. (The loop in the photograph is tied with a water knot from page 116.)

Bring one half of the loop through the other half and tighten by pulling on the lower half. As you tighten the hitch, work the knot that ties the webbing or cord into a loop to the side of the loop, not at the bottom where it could get in the way.

HALF HITCH

THE SIMPLEST AND MOST OFTEN USED HITCH

The half hitch quickly ties a rope to a rail, bar, post, ring, or other object. It comes untied easily—and that could be good or bad. Despite its name, this is actually a complete hitch, often used in the working end of a rope to back up and secure another knot that has already been tied. It is seen most often as part of a more complicated knot, but it can be used alone for simple jobs that do not require the knot to be very strong.

Drape the working end over or through the object to which the rope will be fastened.

Bring the working end back out and over the standing part and then through the loop created. Tighten by pulling simultaneously on the working end and standing part.

VANISHING KNOT

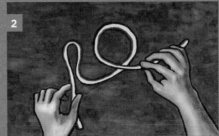

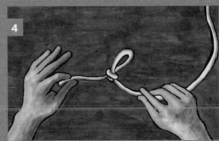

1. Create a circle in your rope.

2. Create a loop to the left of the circle.

3. Tuck the loop into the circle.

4. Holding on to the loop, gently pull to get the circle to wrap tightly around the loop.

5. Pull both ends to make the knot disappear!

HEAVING LINE KNOT

A LARGE STOPPER KNOT THAT ADDS A LOT OF WEIGHT TO THE END OF A ROPE

The weight of the heaving line knot makes it useful for throwing the end of a rope over a long distance. Say you're trying to throw a rope over the limb of a tree so you can hang something from the limb. This knot works great. When a heavy rope needs to be strung across a gap, the heaving line knot can be tied in the end of a lighter line, which in turn is tied to the heavier line. You can throw the lighter line more easily over the gap, and the heavier line can then be drawn (or heaved) behind it.

Form a loop in the working end of a rope. Bring the working end over the standing part and back under the loop.

Bring the working end back over the loop, compressing the loop.

Cat's-Cradle

Cat's-cradle is a game that involves the weaving of a loop of string through one's fingers and hands. Cat's-cradle is one of the oldest games in human history and one of the most widely played games in the world! Variations on this game can be found in Africa, Japan, Australia, America, and the Philippines. Native Americans often called it "web weaving." The game involves one or more players who take turns creating new designs from the original "cat's-cradle."

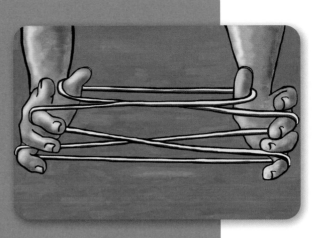

Make three more turns with the working end around the loop.

After the final turn, bring the working end through the loop, holding the turns around the loop as tight as possible. Tighten the knot by pulling on the working end and the standing part. As the turns tighten, form the knot into its final shape.

HIGHWAYMAN'S HITCH

A HITCH FOR SITUATIONS WHERE A QUICK RELEASE MIGHT BE NEEDED

When a temporary hitch is needed, such as when you moor a small boat for a short amount of time, the highwayman's hitch (also known as a draw hitch) does an excellent job. It works well for lowering light loads, like lowering a gear bag over the side of a cliff or off a building. Whether or not it was used by highwaymen (robbers) as a quick-release tether for horses, when a fast getaway was part of the job, is not known, but it works well for temporarily tethering animals. As a bonus, it can be tied in the middle of a line and released from a distance. Don't use this one if you really need to be safe. It can fall apart if the rope is loose and gets shaken.

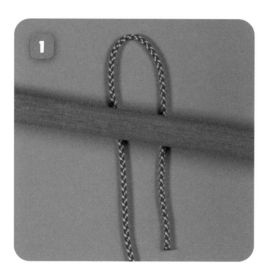

Form a loop in the working end of the rope and hold it behind the attachment point. A long working end will be needed to complete this knot.

Form a second loop in the working end and hold it over the front of the attachment point.

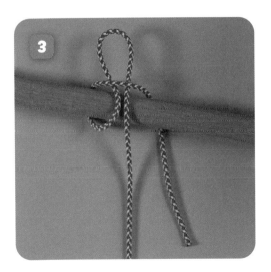

Pass the second loop through the first loop.

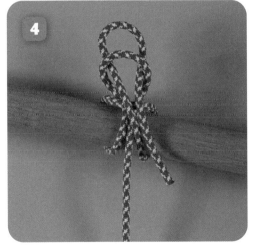

Form a third loop in the working end of the rope, and take this in front of the attachment point and through the second loop, leaving enough of a tail on the working end to easily grab. Tighten by holding the third loop in place while pulling on the standing part. With a quick tug on the working end, the knot falls completely apart.

HUNTER'S BEND

USED FOR JOINING TWO ROPES IN A TIGHT, STRONG, AND SECURE-WHEN-LOADED KNOT

You tie this knot by weaving two overhand knots together. The hunter's bend is quick and easy to learn. It tightens securely when you pull on it, but it can be worked loose when the load is off. This bend works great any time you need to tie the ends of two ropes to each other. Some people call it the rigger's bend.

Tie an overhand knot at the working end of the first rope, but do not tighten it.

Thread the working end of the second rope through the loop of the overhand knot in the first rope. Bring the end of the second rope around and back through the loop of the first overhand a second time, forming an overhand knot in the second rope, as shown in the photograph. Tighten.

INTERLOCKING LOOPS

A KNOT USED TO JOIN TWO PIECES OF CORDAGE USING LOOPS TIED IN THE WORKING ENDS

Interlocking loops can be tied in any material of any size. (As an example, fly-fishing line is shown in the photographs.) They remove the strain on the actual knots that form the loops so you end up with a strong connection between two ropes, lines, or cords. You need to tie these right or one line can cut through the other. The loops must interlock to form a square knot (see page 102), *not* a girth hitch (see page 63).

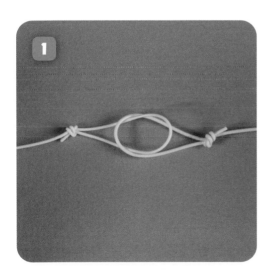 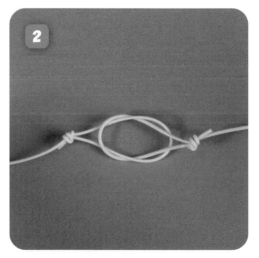

Tie a loop in the working end of both lines. (Many knots will work to create the loops. An overhand on a bight is used in the photographs.) Lay one loop inside the other, as shown in the photograph.

Bring the knot of the outer loop, and the rest of that line, through the inner loop.

KILLICK HITCH

A VARIATION OF THE TIMBER HITCH THAT PROVIDES MORE SECURITY

This is a timber hitch (see page 106) with an additional half hitch. When moving a heavy object, especially by dragging or towing (even through water), the killick hitch holds a rope to an object with more security than a timber hitch. This knot works well if the object to be moved is long. Small boats sometimes use this hitch to attach oddly shaped and heavy objects to the boat to use as an anchor.

Tie a timber hitch (see page 106) around the object to be moved.

At some distance down the rope, add a half hitch around the object, as shown in the photograph.

KLEMHEIST KNOT

A FRICTION KNOT FOR ASCENDING A ROPE

When tied the right way, the klemheist knot (or Machard knot) grips the rope when weighted but releases and slides along the rope when the load is off. It releases and slides with more ease than the Prusik knot (see page 92) but it grips the rope with less strength than the Prusik.

You'll need a loop of rope or a sling of webbing. Wrap the loop or sling four or five times around the rope and toward the load, keeping the wraps neatly laid against the rope.

Pass the lower end of the loop through the upper end of the loop. If you have a carabiner, it's a great way to clip something, such as you, to the rope. (You can add more wraps if the knot slips.)

KNIFE LANYARD KNOT

THIS KNOT CREATES A FIXED LOOP THAT YOU CAN HANG A KNIFE OR OTHER OBJECT FROM

A lanyard is a cord, or maybe a strap, that lets you carry something around your neck or over a shoulder. This knot is tied to create a lanyard from a piece of cordage. Even though it's called a knife lanyard knot, you can hang many things from it. Depending on the object to be hung from the lanyard, sometimes the item must be strung onto the cord prior to the tying of the knot, like if you wanted to put a key on your lanyard. Though it appears complex to tie, it's really not that difficult; just have patience tightening the knot. What will you tie to your lanyard?

Drape the cord over your left hand as shown in the photograph. Make a loop in the end of the cord (as shown) and hold the loop between your thumb and index finger (as shown). Important: The loop behind your hand will be the final loop.

Bring the end indicated in the photograph (the end hanging down to the left side in the step 1 photo) up through the loop in your palm as shown in the photograph.

Weaverbirds make their nests using their beaks and feet and tie real knots from grass, roots, twigs, and leaves!

Bring the same end through the knot again as shown in the photograph.

Bring the other end through the knot as shown in the photograph. Slip the arrangement off your hand and meticulously work the knot into its final form.

LOOP KNOT

THE QUICKEST AND SIMPLEST LOOP IN THE MIDDLE OF A ROPE

When something needs to be attached mid-rope, the loop knot works great. This knot is important because you can also use it to keep using a damaged rope. With the damaged part in the middle of the knot, at the top of the loop, the damaged part is not being used. Using a knot to "strengthen" a damaged rope is an emergency measure to prevent the rope from breaking. Any damaged rope needs to be replaced. And also be warned: The loop knot is not designed to bear a lot of weight. For a serious weight-bearing mid-rope knot, use the alpine butterfly (see page 2).

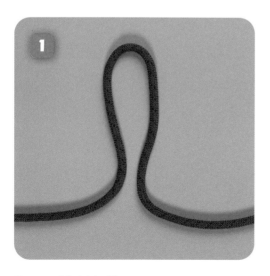

Form a bight in the rope.

Tie an overhand knot (see page 85) in the bight. Tighten by pulling slowly on the loop and the main section of the rope.

Gordian Knot

According to Greek folklore, the Gordian knot was an impossibly complicated knot, tied to an old oxcart, thought to have been created by the ancient king and founder of Gordius. Roman historian Quintus Curtius Rufus described the knot as "having several knots all so tightly entangled that it was impossible to see how they were fastened." A prophet foretold that the person who could untie the Gordian knot would someday become the king of Asia. Centuries later, in 333 BC, Alexander the Great visited Gordium and attempted to untie the impossible knot, but had no success. He then decided that it made no difference how the knot was untied, and he drew his sword and in one forceful swoop cut the knot in half! He later conquered Asia and fulfilled the prophecy! Today, the metaphor "to cut the Gordian knot" means to solve a challenging problem with a single bold stroke.

MIDSHIPMAN'S HITCH

A SLIDE-AND-GRIP LOOP FOR SUSPENDING OBJECTS OR ADDING TENSION TO A LINE

The midshipman's hitch, like a lot of misnamed knots, is not really a hitch. This knot is a slide-and-grip *loop* that can be moved on the rope after being tied. When a load is applied to this knot, it pinches the standing part of the line at enough of an angle to cause the knot to grip firmly. When the load is off, the knot slides freely. If the working end is left long enough, a stopper knot can be tied around the standing part of the line, giving this knot a semipermanent position on the line. "Semipermanent" means it won't slide anymore until you untie the stopper.

TWO-PERSON KNOT GAME (2 PLAYERS)

Using a 10-foot-long rope, you and your buddy each hold a piece of the rope in your right hand. Together attempt to tie a square knot without letting go of the rope.

Form a loop in the working end of the rope.

Take the working end around the standing part and up through the loop.

Take the working end around the standing part and up through the loop a second time, taking care to make the second turn overlap the first turn as shown in the photograph.

With the working end, tie a half hitch (see page 64) around the standing part above the loop. The knot can be moved to adjust the size of the loop. When it is tightened and the loop loaded, the knot will grip.

MONKEY'S FIST

A LARGE, ROUND DECORATIVE KNOT WITH PRACTICAL USES

If you use your imagination, the monkey's fist does resemble a fist—sort of. It's probably the most famous decorative knot. It was probably developed by sailors who needed a heavy heaving line knot and who sometimes tied it around a stone or iron ball to add weight. The knot can be tied around a rubber ball if you want the knot to float.

Decoratively, the monkey's fist is popular as a large and attractive end to any cord, especially if the cord will be used as a pull-string. It is most often tied as a two-ply or three-ply knot. (A three-ply knot is illustrated here.) It can be tied larger than a three-ply. In addition to being tied around a spherical object (a marble or golf ball would work fine for small jobs), it can be tied around your hand as a starting point; this is known as the sailor's method and is shown here. Yes, it's a little tricky to tie the first time—and maybe the second time—but it's always a lot of fun to know this knot.

Wrap the cord around your hand as shown in the photograph.

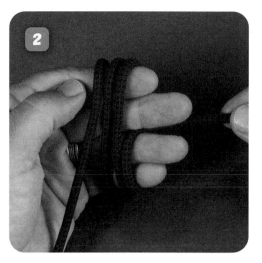

Trap the final wrap with your fingers as shown.

Slip the upper half of the wraps off your fingers and continue to wrap an equal number of wraps around the first set of wraps, as shown in the photograph. A spherical object may be inserted at this point.

With the bundle entirely off your fingers, make a third set of wraps, the same in number, around and through where the two bundles of cord meet. It will take some time to tighten and form the ball into its final spherical shape. Be sure to tuck the end inside the knot to hide it.

COOL SPIRAL MACRAME BRACELETS

The spiral half knot is a fun "twist" on the square knot (see page 102). When creating a traditional square knot pattern, you take turns using "knotters" from the left and right side. The result is an interesting flat pattern that makes for a nice bracelet, choker, or macrame design.

The spiral half knot is very similar. It's created by repeatedly using just a half knot, or an incomplete square knot, which always starts at the same side. So, instead of switching back and forth, the knotters always start from the same direction, which creates a fun spiral effect.

1. Start with two strands of 70-inch-long cords. Fold each cord in half and tie two cow hitch knots over a stick or dowel to secure them. The cords on the left and right edges are called working cords or "knotters." The strands in the middle are called "filler" cords.

2. Take the left knotter and bring it over the two fillers and under the right knotter.

3. Take the right knotter, bring it over the left knotter, under the filler cords, and pass it through the left loop.

Variation: Try repeating the square knot for a different effect. Instead of starting each knot from the same side, take turns starting with knotters from different sides. If you start the knot on the left, the next knot will start from the right. Go back and forth until you have the length you want. For fun you can string beads through the two filler cords at different points in your design. Make sure you find beads with extra-large holes so the strings can fit through them.

4. Gently, but firmly, pull your knotter cords toward the dowel holding the filler cords still. Repeat the knot from the same side as the first.

5. As you continue making the same knot, you will notice it naturally starts to spiral! When you get the length you desire, tie the ends together. You're done!

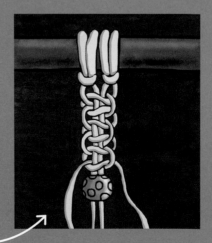

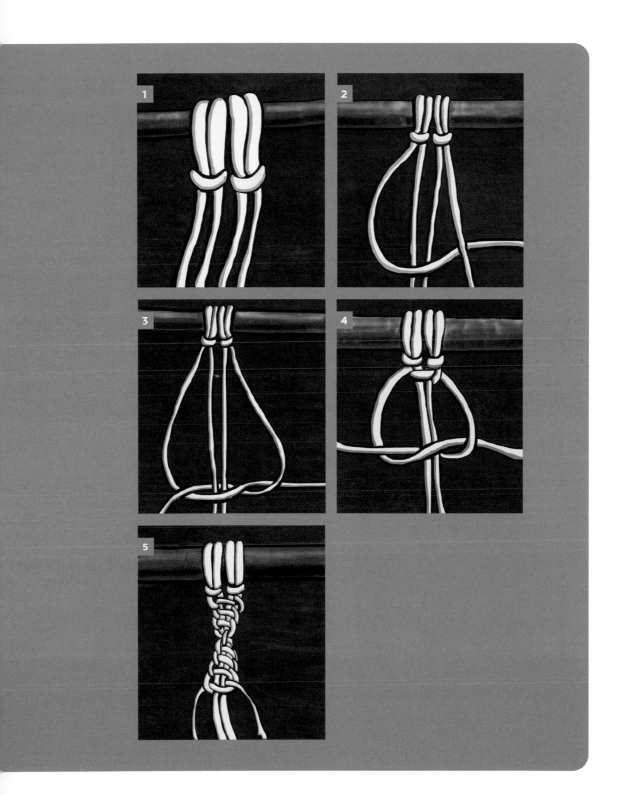

MUNTER HITCH

USED FOR IMPROVISING A BELAY OR A RAPPEL DEVICE WITH THE USE OF ONE OR TWO CARABINERS

The Munter hitch (sometimes called the Italian hitch) is a clever little knot that works as a climbing device for belaying and rappelling. If you're not a climber, you might skip this one. The knot grips a carabiner when a load is applied, but the rope runs through the carabiner when the load is off. It should be used with one locking carabiner or two non-locking carabiners with the gates reversed. The photo shows a locking carabiner. Test the knot on safe ground by pulling aggressively on the standing part before trusting it to save a life!

Twist a coil into the rope with the upper and lower strands of the coil folded together, as shown in the photograph.

Clip the carabiner into both sides of the folded strands with the spine of the carabiner next to the strand that will bear the load.

OVERHAND KNOT

A SIMPLE AND USEFUL STOPPER KNOT THAT ALSO FORMS THE BASIS FOR MANY MORE COMPLEX KNOTS

This is a small knot, and it's just about everybody's first knot. You often tie it by accident—like in your shoelaces. One reason you need to know this one is because it is the start of a lot of larger knots. When it gets pulled tight, the overhand knot can be very difficult to untie. So keep a lookout for one in your rope or cord where you don't want it. Remove an unwanted overhand as soon as possible.

Create a loop in the working end of a rope or cord.

Take the working end over the standing part and back up through the loop. Tighten the knot by pulling simultaneously on the working end and the standing end.

OVERHAND DOUBLE KNOT

A COMPACT STOPPER FOR SMALL- TO LARGE-DIAMETER CORD OR LINE

Not only a simple and useful stopper knot, the overhand double knot (or double overhand) works in all sizes of material, from thin thread to thick cord. It shows up as a basis for other knots, including bends, and can be tied in the end of lines to prevent fraying. It is an essential knot to know.

Tie an overhand knot (see page 85) in the working end.

Tuck the working end through the loop of the overhand a second time. Tighten by pulling gently on both ends. As the knot begins to tighten, twist both ends of the knot in opposite directions with your fingers. Continue to tighten to give the knot its characteristic shape.

OVERHAND KNOT WITH DRAW LOOP

A VARIATION OF THE OVERHAND KNOT THAT IS SLIGHTLY LARGER AND MUCH EASIER TO UNTIE

When a simple overhand knot is tightened over a loop, you can draw the loop out easily by holding the knot and pulling on the working end. This makes the overhand knot with draw loop a better choice than the basic overhand when your knot will be untied soon or often.

Tie an overhand knot (see page 85) in the working end of a rope or cord.

Before tightening the knot, take the working end back through the overhand. Tighten the knot by pulling on the loop with one hand and the working end and standing part with the other hand.

OVERHAND LOOP

A SIMPLE AND SECURE FIXED LOOP FOR USE WITH STRING OR LIGHT CORD

Almost as simple as the basic overhand knot (see page 85), the overhand loop creates a quick and useful knot. This knot can be tied in the middle of a rope if a loop is needed there. It also offers another advantage: If a rope has a worn or weak point, you can make the weak point a part of the loop, making the rope stronger. But be warned: This knot can jam when tied in rope. Prevent jamming by keeping the knot from being too heavily loaded, especially a sudden and strong jerk on the rope.

Make a relatively long bight in the working end of the cord.

Tie an overhand knot (see page 85) with the doubled cord.

PILE (POST) HITCH

A QUICK, SIMPLE, AND SECURE ATTACHMENT TO PILE, POST, OR STAKE

The pile hitch (or post hitch) is really simple and really useful. And it can be tied anywhere in a rope, even the middle. By tying the knot in the middle of a rope, the rope can be pulled in two directions from the knot, making this great for putting up a barrier rope between a line of posts. It has numerous other uses, such as tying a tent line to a stake. It unties very easily.

Double the section of line to be attached and wrap it around the pile or post.

Take the loop over the top of the pile or post, then pull on the standing part to tighten. Note: The knot can be pushed down the pile or post before being tightened.

POLE HITCH

THIS KNOT TIES LONG OBJECTS TOGETHER

Poles, paddles, oars, and any long objects (including long-handled tools such as brooms and rakes) can be held together with the pole hitch. This makes them easier to carry and easier to store. If the long objects are really long, you can use two pole hitches. This knot is easier to manage when the length of rope or cord being used is just long enough to do the job.

ONE-HANDED KNOT GAME (1+ PLAYERS)
This is a game to be played alone or with friends. The object of the game is to see if you can tie an overhand knot using only one hand. Place a 20-inch rope evenly over your wrist. Using only one hand, attempt to tie an overhand knot.

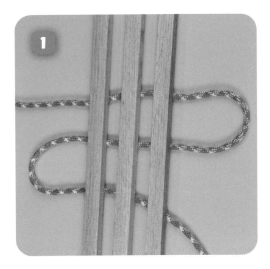

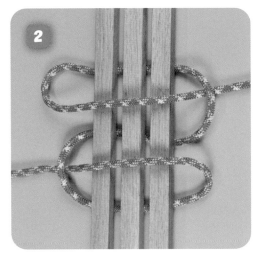

Arrange the cord beneath the long objects in an S or Z shape.

Bring the ends of the rope over the objects and through the opposite bights, as shown in the photograph.

Draw the objects together, bringing both ends of the rope to the same side of the objects, as shown in the photograph.

Secure the ends with a square knot (see page 102).

PRUSIK KNOT

A FRICTION KNOT USED FOR ASCENDING A ROPE

A Prusik knot slides up the rope when unloaded but grips the rope firmly when loaded, so it is actually a slide-and-grip hitch. And it grips the rope with a lot of strength. In fact, a Prusik can be difficult to break free after being loaded with a heavy weight. But it can be broken free by loosening the "tongue" (center loop) first. This knot is a better choice for new, wet, or otherwise slippery rope. You can also tie a Prusik to a rope so you can hang something from the rope.

Tie a loop in a cord of significantly smaller diameter than the main rope.

Attach the loop to the main rope with a girth hitch (see page 63), keeping the hitch loose.

"Tying the knot" is an idiom or expression that refers to the union of two people in marriage. Even today, in some religious ceremonies, sashes, cords, or ribbons are placed around the hands of the couple. In medieval times, when a couple became engaged, they would tie their hands together to declare their intention to marry, usually within a year.

Bring the loop around the rope and back through the hitch a second time.

Bring the loop around and through a third time. Lay the wraps of loop evenly and without twists to maximize the bite on the rope. Tighten the knot against the rope. Test the knot, and if it slips when you don't want it to, add more wraps.

ROLLING HITCH

A HITCH FOR SITUATIONS WHERE THE LOAD WILL BE APPLIED AT AN ANGLE TO THE KNOT OTHER THAN A RIGHT ANGLE

Many hitches can fall apart when you pull on the rope in a direction other than a right angle. The rolling hitch, one of the basic knots, does not fall apart as long as the pull on the rope is fairly steady. You can use this hitch to "hitch" a rope to just about anything. In the photographs, a rolling hitch is used to tie a rope to a rope.

With the working end, make two turns around the object or around the larger line.

Take the working end back up over the standing part. Make another turn around the object or larger line from underneath, and bring the working end out underneath itself (as shown in the photograph). Tighten the turns by pulling on the working end and the standing part simultaneously. When the load is applied, the knot grips the object or line.

ROUND TURN AND TWO HALF HITCHES

A VARIATION OF TWO HALF HITCHES THAT CREATES A KNOT OF SUPER STRENGTH

This basic knot is one of the simplest and most useful knots ever. Not only strong and dependable, this knot when tied correctly never jams. Because weight applied to the standing part pulls the rope in a straight line, you do not lose any of the strength of the rope with a round turn and two half hitches.

Take the working end of the rope around an object in a full round turn.

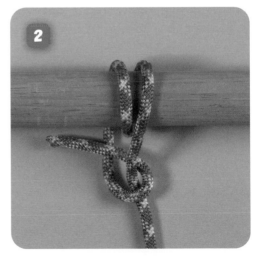

Tie two half hitches (see page 64) in the working end. Remember to tighten the first half hitch before tying the second.

SCAFFOLD KNOT

A STRONG BUT SIMPLE SLIDING LOOP

This knot is more complex than the slipknot. The scaffold knot is a sturdy loop that slides to fit snugly around a bar, rail, or other object. This knot can be used any time you want a sliding loop more secure than the slipknot. It is often used by fishermen to secure a hook to the end of fishing line.

OVER THE MOUNTAIN (3+ PLAYERS)
Two players sit on chairs holding the ends of a rope about 20 feet apart. The seated players lower the rope between them to about 1 foot off the ground so the other players can hop over it. After each round the rope is lifted higher and the players attempt to jump over the new, more challenging heights. Players are eliminated when their feet touch the rope.

Form a loop in the working end of the line, then bring the working end around the back of the standing part.

Bring the working end back across the top of the loop.

Bring the working end around the back of the standing part a second time, as shown in the photograph.

Take the working end up through both loops and tighten by pulling on the working end and the loop. Be sure the turns around the line lay down neatly against each other.

SHEEPSHANK KNOT

A KNOT FOR SHORTENING ANY LINE TO THE LENGTH YOU WANT

With the sheepshank, you can shorten a rope without cutting it. It ties and unties easily. As long as someone or something is pulling on the rope, this knot stays put. But when you pull on the sheepshank, it must be done slowly and cautiously, because this knot can fall apart easily. So fully tighten the knot and apply the load (the tension) gradually rather than suddenly.

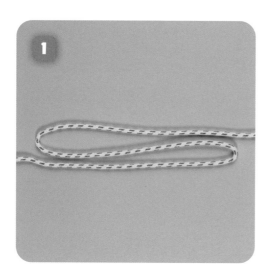

Lay out two bights (see page 16) in the line in an S or Z shape.

Use the main line to tie two half hitches (see page 64) over the ends of both bights as shown in the photograph. (You can make your sheepshank stronger by tying two half hitches on both ends.) Slowly pull on both the main parts of the line, taking care to keep the knot in its proper shape and form. The two loops at the ends of the knot need to stay approximately the same size.

SHEET BEND

A QUICK AND SIMPLE BEND FOR TYING TOGETHER TWO ROPES OR CORDS OF EQUAL OR UNEQUAL DIAMETER

This is another basic knot and probably the most commonly used bend. It's called the sheet bend, and it works well in lines of unequal diameter. The strength of this knot, however, goes down when the difference in the size of the two ropes or cords is a big difference. If the ropes are unequal in diameter, make the bight in the larger rope, and it will be more secure if both working ends emerge on the same side of the knot. Take a look at the pictures for a better understanding.

Create a bight (see page 16) in the working end of one of the two ropes.

Bring the working end of the second rope through the bight, then around the back of the bight and across the top of the bight. Then bring it underneath itself and over the other rope, as shown in the photograph. Tighten by pulling on both standing parts.

SHEET BEND DOUBLE

A REINFORCED VERSION OF THE SHEET BEND THAT PROVIDES GREATER SECURITY

When you really want the knot to stay tied, use the sheet bend double (or double sheet bend) instead of the sheet bend. It is a strong knot even when the ropes are wet and even when the load on the ropes is heavy. This is especially true when the ropes are of unequal diameter.

Tie two ropes together with a sheet bend (see page 99).

Bring the working end of the second rope around the bight in the first rope a second time before tucking it under itself, as shown in the photograph of the finished knot. Be sure the turns lie neatly beside each other before tightening.

SLIPKNOT (SIMPLE SLIDING LOOP)

THE SIMPLEST OF SLIDING LOOPS THAT TIGHTENS WHEN PULLED

The slipknot (also known as the simple sliding loop) slides along the rope so you can make the loop smaller or bigger. This knot is like an overhand knot with draw loop. But, in an overhand knot with draw loop, the working end forms the loop. In a slipknot, the standing part forms the loop.

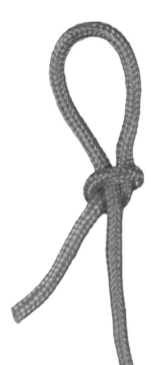

Tie an overhand knot (see page 85) near the working end of a rope or cord.

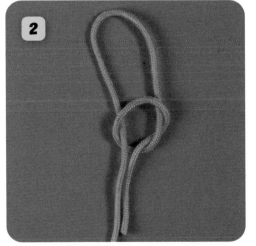

Pull the standing part up, over, and through the loop of the overhand knot. Tighten by pulling simultaneously on the loop created in the standing part and the working end.

SQUARE KNOT

A QUICK AND SIMPLE BEND FOR TYING TOGETHER TWO ROPES OR CORDS OF EQUAL DIAMETER

This knot is most often called the square knot, but it's sometimes called the reef knot. It is used for tying together two pieces of cordage of equal diameter or two ends of the same piece of cordage. If improperly tied, as it often is, it becomes the famous (and not very useful) granny knot. Even tied correctly, the square knot loosens easily and should not be used as a bend when you really need for it to stay tied.

Bring the two working ends of the two pieces of cordage together and cross them left over right.

Cross the two working ends a second time, right over left. Tighten by pulling simultaneously on both working ends and both standing parts.

Macrame Knots

Macrame is an artistic form of knot making that is thought to have been developed by Arab weavers in the thirteenth century to decoratively finish the excess yarn remaining on the fringes of veils, towels, and shawls. The word is derived from the Arabic word *migramah*, meaning ornamental fringe or embroidered veil. After the Moorish conquest, macrame was brought to Spain and then spread throughout Europe. Sailors enjoyed making macrame objects while at sea and further spread the art to the New World and China. It became very popular in the Victorian era as decoration on curtains, tablecloths, and bedspreads. The United States saw a revival of this art in the 1970s, when it frequently appeared on wall hangings, clothing, plant hangers, and jewelry.

TAUTLINE HITCH

THIS KNOT LETS YOU TAKE UP SLACK IN A ROPE OR CORD

The tautline hitch creates a tight (or taut) line with a simple knot. It's sort of like the trucker's hitch (see page 110), but it's easier to tie. It's not a bad choice when you want to make a tent line tight between the tent and the tent stake. The knot slides freely but jams against the rope or cord it is tied around when a load is applied. You can make more tension with a trucker's hitch, and the trucker's hitch is more secure, so you'll probably end up choosing a trucker's hitch more often. And the tautline hitch will loosen if slack develops in the rope, so you need to check it often.

Take the working end around or through a secure or tie-down point (such as the ring in the photograph) and back under the standing part to form a loop.

With the working end, make two or three turns around the standing part within the loop, as shown in the photograph.

FUN FACT

Did you know that there's a branch of mathematics called *knot theory*? Knot theory mathematicians study and classify knots that have their ends joined together. The simplest of these is called the "unknot," which is simply a ring.

Bring the working end down and underneath the standing part outside the loop, as shown in the photograph, forming a second loop.

Take the working end through the second loop and tighten by pulling on the standing part. The knot can now be pushed up the standing part, taking slack out of the rope. Under pressure, the knot grips and holds against the standing part, maintaining tension in the rope.

TIMBER HITCH

TEMPORARILY ATTACHES A ROPE TO AN OBJECT FOR DRAGGING, RAISING, OR LOWERING

A basic knot, the timber hitch serves as a short-term sliding loop, quickly tying a rope to a heavy object that needs to be moved by pulling, dragging, lifting, or lowering. It is very secure under tension and never jams. But be careful: Those new to knots often tie this one incorrectly, and then the knot fails. So be careful. The timber hitch can also loosen and fail if there is too much slack in the rope, or if you pull and let go, pull and let go.

Pass the working end around the object to be moved and then behind and around the standing part.

Twist the working end around itself (not around the standing part) at least three times. The number of twists can be increased to boost the grip of the knot, depending on the size and weight of the object. Tighten by pulling on the standing part.

Guinness World Records

Did you know you can get into Guinness World Records for your knot tying skills? Here are some awards you might try to beat:

- In 1999, Al Gliniecki tied 39 cherry stems into knots in only 3 minutes using only his tongue!
- Tying the "tightest knot structure" ever goes to researchers at the University of Manchester, UK, for tightly braiding tiny strands of molecules to 2.5 nanometers per crossing. (A nanometer is a measurement of length that is one billionth of a meter—very, very small!)
- The record for the fastest tying of six knots from the *Boy Scout Handbook* was won by Clinton Bailey in 1977, who completed this feat in 8.1 seconds!
- In 2017, Deepak Sharma, also known as Mr. Tie Man, tied a Windsor knot necktie in only 12.89 seconds.
- The Junior Chamber of International Japan Kyoto Bloc Council (phew!) in 2019 won the award for the largest human knot, consisting of 123 participants!
- The most knots *undone* by a dog was won by Gustl, a Terrier mix who untied ten knots in less than one minute.
- The largest Chinese knot ever created was about 133 feet by 136 feet and weighed four tons. It took two months for kindergarteners, parents, and teachers to create this giant knot.

TRANSOM KNOT

A USEFUL KNOT FOR TYING TOGETHER TWO CROSSED PIECES OF RIGID MATERIAL

When you want to tie two things together, the transom knot (called by some the strangle knot) is very useful. It's a great knot for securing a pole between two trees. Then you can hang things from the pole. It works well in light cord to bind together light pieces of wood, such as when you make a kite or garden trellis, and it holds nicely in synthetic or natural-fiber cord. It is similar to but slightly less complex than the constrictor knot (see page 35). This knot is typically tied in short pieces of rope or cordage, because longer pieces are hard to work with.

HOT LAVA ROPE WALK (2+ PLAYERS)

Imagine you are walking on a very narrow path surrounded by hot lava! If you fall off the path, you fall into the hot lava! Oh no!

There are different ways to play this game, depending on your skills, but all require you to lay a long piece of rope or string on the ground to represent the path. The first method is to simply walk forward on the rope without falling off (into the lava). If you're feeling brave, you can walk backward on the rope or lay the rope in different patterns to increase the difficulty level.

With the working end of the rope, make a loop around the vertical piece of rigid material.

Take the working end across the horizontal piece of rigid material and completely around the vertical piece below the horizontal piece, as shown in the photograph.

Cross the horizontal piece a second time. Take the working end underneath itself where it crosses the horizontal piece.

Take the working end underneath the standing part where it forms part of the original loop (as shown in the photograph) and tighten by pulling on both ends of the rope.

TRUCKER'S HITCH

A KNOT THAT TAKES UP SLACK IN A ROPE OR CORD

The trucker's hitch is more accurately described as a system of knots giving a three-to-one mechanical advantage that allows tension to be created in a rope or cord. This knot, in other words, works like a pulley, allowing more tension to be created than by simply pulling on the end of the rope. A rope can be drawn as tight as a guitar string, if needed, but the amount of tension is under the control of you, the knot tyer. This knot is an excellent method of keeping a tent line tight between a tent and a tent stake. It also works well for securing gear to the top of a vehicle or anything in the back of a truck.

First, tie a quick-release loop, such as an overhand loop (see page 88), an appropriate distance from the working end of the rope or cord. Then pass the working end through the tie-down point (a ring in the photograph, for example).

Bring the working end through the quick-release loop.

Gorillas and orangutans have been known to make knots often for nest building in nature and for fun in captivity!

Pull the working end toward the tie-down point to create the amount of tension required.

When appropriate tension is in the rope or cord, secure the knot with a half hitch (see page 64), or an overhand knot with draw loop (see page 87), as shown in the photograph.

TWO HALF HITCHES

A VARIATION OF THE HALF HITCH THAT CREATES A MORE SECURE KNOT

Two half hitches will hold a rope to an object or another rope with twice the security of a single half hitch. Security is lost, however, if the load is not applied at a right angle to the object (see how the rope runs straight from the knot in the picture). The knot is a half hitch tied on top of a half hitch. If there is no load on the rope (if there is not a constant pull on the rope), this knot will work loose.

Fasten a rope to an object with a half hitch (see page 64). Tighten the half hitch.

Take the working end around again, over the standing part again, and through the loop a second time. Tighten by pulling simultaneously on the working end and the standing part.

Name Those Knots

1) Alpine Butterfly, 2) Monkey's Fist, 3) Chain Sinnet (Monkey Chain), 4) Rolling Hitch, 5) Hunter's Bend, 6) Overhand Loop, 7) Zeppelin Bend, 8) Vice Versa, 9) Bowline on a Bight, 10) Prusik Knot, 11) Figure 8 Knot, 12) Fisherman's Knot

KNOTS FOR KIDS • 113

VICE VERSA

A KNOT USED FOR JOINING TWO LINES TOGETHER EVEN WHEN THEY ARE WET AND SLIPPERY

Slick lines, such as polyethylene or even strips of wet leather, can be tied together firmly with the vice versa. It's not super easy to tie the first time or two. But you'll get it—after you practice. But beware: If the two working ends are not woven together exactly as shown, the final knot will not be a true vice versa, and the knot may completely fail.

ROPE LIMBO (3+ PLAYERS)
Two players take the end of the rope and start by raising it high to allow other players to pass under it. As the rope is lowered at each pass, players must bend backward with their backs facing the ground. No part of the body can touch the rope as the player moves under, and only their feet are allowed to touch the ground. After each pass, the players attempt to pass under the rope again, until the rope gets too low and they can't pass under it anymore.

Lay the two lines alongside each other, the working ends pointing in opposite directions. Loop each line around the other, as shown in the photograph.

Bring the working end of one line through the loop in the other line (from back to front), as shown in the photograph.

Continue to weave the two lines together by bringing the second working end through the loop in the other line (from back to front), as shown in the photograph.

Work the knot into its distinctive shape as it is tightened, as shown in the photograph.

WATER KNOT

JOINS TWO ENDS OF TUBULAR NYLON WEBBING

Webbing is nylon woven stoutly into a tubular shape, then flattened. You can tie two ends of a piece of webbing together to form a loop. Or you can tie two ends of separate pieces of webbing together to make one longer piece. When you tie ends of webbing together, the water knot is your best choice. It is tied by weaving two overhand knots together, one the mirror image of the other. (You can use a water knot to tie things like rope and fishing line together, too, but it is the best knot to use with webbing.) When you pull this knot tight, really tight, it can be very difficult to untie.

Form an overhand knot in the end of the webbing, making sure the webbing is arranged to allow the knot to lie flat if pressed.

Slide the second end of webbing into the first overhand knot, as if you're tracing the knot. Start at the point where the first end of webbing leaves the first overhand knot, as shown in the photograph.

FUN FACT

Knots can be found in the DNA of our body's cells. Scientists study these knots to understand why they tangle and how to untangle them.

Continue to follow the lead of the first piece of webbing through the overhand knot with the second end of webbing, making sure both ends of webbing lie flat against each other.

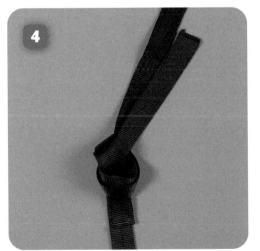

When both ends of webbing have been woven into one overhand knot, tighten it by pulling on the working ends of the webbing. Before trusting the knot to stop a fall, load it with body weight to set it as tight as possible.

WHIPPING (COMMON)

USED TO PREVENT A ROPE OF SEVERAL STRANDS FROM FRAYING

Whipping is the process of wrapping the end of a rope or line with strong, thin twine to prevent fraying (coming apart). A frayed end is difficult to use and can lead to loss of a piece of your rope. When a rope is to be cut, always take steps to prevent fraying before cutting. Synthetic twine should be used on synthetic rope and natural-fiber twine on natural-fiber ropes. This common whipping is far from the most secure whipping, but it will work until you can find a more dependable whipping, usually something sewn onto the rope.

PHYSICAL FITNESS KNOT RACE (2+ PLAYERS)
Each player is given a 3-foot piece of cord. Open this book to a random page that everyone can see. Players race to see who can tie the knot on the page first. The one who finishes first gets to choose the fitness exercise for the group and how many reps you will do. Exercises might include jumping jacks, push-ups, sit-ups, squats, lunges, running, cartwheels, skipping, forward lunges, touching toes, stretching, or make up your own! Repeat with the next knot.

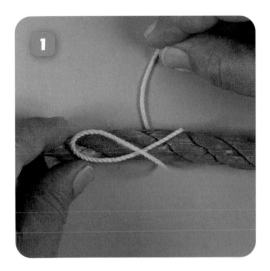

Lay a loop (or bight) of twine along the rope near the end.

Wrap several turns of twine around the loop to bind it to the rope.

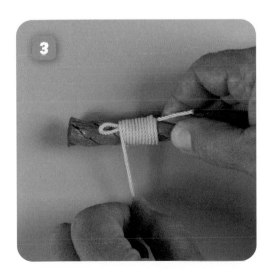

Continue binding the twine to the rope for a width at least a little greater than the diameter of the rope. Make the turns of twine as tight as possible.

Tuck the working end through what is left of the loop and tighten by pulling on the standing part until the loop disappears beneath the binding.

ZEPPELIN BEND

A SECURE KNOT FOR JOINING TWO LINES TOGETHER THAT CAN BE LOADED BEFORE IT IS TIGHTENED

The zeppelin bend can be loaded before the knot is tightened because it will form into its proper shape and work when loaded. This can be a great advantage if, say, you are tying off a boat as the boat is drifting away. As with many knots, there is more than one way to tie a zeppelin bend. This method is old and considered by many to be easier. This knot can also be used by anyone wishing to bend (tie together) two ropes.

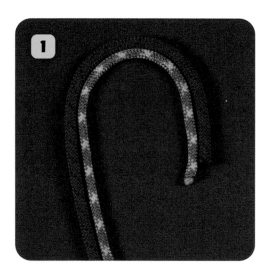

Hold the two working ends alongside each other, both pointing in the same direction, as shown in the photograph.

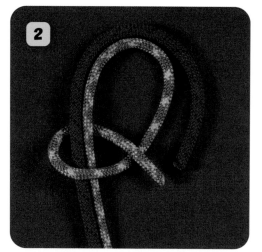

Tie a half hitch (see page 64) in the nearest line so that it encloses the second line, as shown in the photograph.

© Getty Images/View Stock

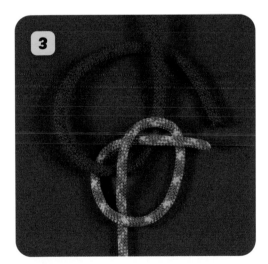

3

Bring the standing part of the second line away from the first line in the opposite direction and across the second working end, as shown in the photograph.

4

Bring the working end of the second line through the loop in the first line and through its own loop (as shown in the photograph), forming two interlocked overhands. As soon as both standing parts are loaded, the knot will assume the proper shape and security.

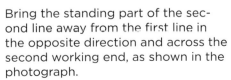

INDEX

ABOUT THE AUTHORS

Buck Tilton is the author of *Knack Knots You Need, Knack Hiking & Backpacking, Knack First Aid,* and *Outward Bound USA Ropes, Knots, and Hitches. H*is many books for FalconGuides, including the award-winning *Wilderness First Responder,* have sold more than 300,000 copies combined. He teaches at Central Wyoming College.

Experienced outdoor chef and artist Christine Conners is the author of the nationally popular Lipsmackin' and Scout outdoor cookbook series. If you'd like to see more of her work across other mediums, visit Christine at lipsmackincampin.com and artbyconners.com.